INTRODUCTION

Disclaimer

This eBook has been written for information purposes only. Every effort has been made to make this eBook as complete and accurate as possible. However, there may be mistakes in typography or content. Also, this eBook provides information only up to the publishing date. Therefore, this eBook should be used as a guide - not as the ultimate source.

The purpose of this eBook is to educate. The author and the publisher do not warrant that the information contained in this eBook is fully complete and shall not be responsible for any errors or omissions. The author and publisher shall have neither liability nor responsibility to any person or entity with respect to any loss or damage caused or alleged to be caused directly or indirectly by this ebook.

This eBook offers information and is designed for educational purposes only. You should not rely on this information as a substitute for, nor does it replace professional medical advice, diagnosis, or treatment.

Table of Contents

INTRODUCTION

Meditation is a great way to reconnect with yourself and calm your body and mind. As a result, meditation comes with several benefits that are helpful to your emotional and physical well-being.

Unfortunately, many people believe that meditation takes up too much time and that they are too busy to do a meditation practice. This is a myth. Anyone, even the busiest people, can and should incorporate meditation into their daily routines in order to experience the full benefits of meditation.

In this guide, we want to help you meditate despite your busy schedule. We will begin by looking at meditation and its benefits. Then, we will discover meditation's effects on the mind and body.

After that, we will go over three meditation techniques for you to try. Lastly, we will help you to create a daily practice that you can use meditation to heal your soul.

After reading this guide, even the busiest person will be able to incorporate meditation into their daily routines and experience the numerous benefits that come with daily meditation.

As you read, we ask you to keep an open mind and pay attention to your reactions. Your reactions will help you to determine the best forms of meditation for your needs and tell you a little about yourself. No matter what, though, stay open to meditation and its possibilities.

CHAPTER 1
WHAT IS MEDITATION?

WHAT IS MEDITATION?

Meditation is loosely defined as a practice used to both train attention and awareness and achieve mental clarity and emotional stability. The practice includes a number of techniques, such as breathing or moving, in order to achieve the goal of heightened attention and emotional stability.

Beyond this loose definition, many scholars have struggled to define the phenomenon more precisely. The reason for this is that meditation comes in several forms and is incorporated differently into religious and non-religious settings. Let's look at what meditation is more closely.

History

Meditation has been practiced since 1500 BCE. The earliest records of meditation are seen in the Hindu traditions of Vendantism, which is a form of Hinduism that still utilizes meditation today. Other forms of early meditation were developed by Taoists in China and Buddhists in India.

Early Jews and Christians also tried meditative practices. Philo of Alexandria and Plotinus are two Jewish and Christian thinkers who specifically wrote about meditation around 20 BCE, but their views were not fully accepted into their respective religions until the Middle Ages.

During the Middle Ages, meditation became more integrated with Western religions, such as Christianity, Judaism, and Islam. Lectio Divina, Kabbalistic practices, and Sufism are just three examples of meditation becoming more intertwined with Western religious faith during the Middle Ages. At the same time, meditative practices were brought to Japan, where they further developed and were integrated into other forms of Buddhism.

It was not until the 19th century that meditation began to transform from a religious ritual to a non-spiritual and health-centred practice. This transition occurred whenever Asian meditation techniques spread to the West.

Once they spread, Western meditators found alternative applications for meditation, causing the already difficult to define practice to be even more difficult to define.

Today, meditation is practiced in both spiritual and non-spiritual settings. People of Indian, East Asian, and Abrahamic faiths, for example, often practice spiritual meditation, while business people and Yoga-class attendees often practice non-spiritual meditation.

In both scenarios, though, meditation is treated as a practice that is used to sharpen the brain's ability to focus and add clarity and stability to the mind and emotions.

Meditation Categories

Since the 19th century, meditation has been divided into two broad categories: focused (or concentrative) meditation and open monitoring (or mindfulness) meditation. Each category has its own benefits and applications.

Focused meditation is when you concentrate on a single thing. Paying attention to the breath, a feeling, a koan, or an affirmation are all concentrative meditation techniques. The benefit of this category is that it sharpens your mind and builds your ability to focus on a single thing.

Open monitoring meditation is when you are mindful of your state and surroundings. The benefit of this category is that you are brought to the present as your senses are sharpened and made aware of the states around you.

Some meditative practices use both concentrative meditation and open-monitoring meditation, though. Such practices include vipassana and samatha in their meditations.

It is important to emphasize that focused meditation and open monitoring are just categories of meditation. Within both categories, there are countless meditation styles and techniques.

Meditation elements

Meditation includes a number of elements. Though these elements need not be used in every form of meditation, they tend to make meditation practices more effective and helpful, especially for beginners or busy people.

The most important element of meditation is focused attention. Without this element, it is impossible to practice meditation. Focusing your attention allows you to train your mind and escape from distractions. You can focus your attention by closing your eyes, focusing on an object, or reciting an affirmation.

Another important element of meditation is relaxed breathing. Relaxed breathing includes deep, even-paced, and intentional breathing. The purpose of this element is to take in more oxygen, reduce muscle tension, and experience the benefits of enhanced breathing.

Unless you are practicing a rigorous form of meditation, finding a quiet setting is another powerful element of meditation. Quiet settings will allow you to better escape from the distractions and focus your mind. Some experienced meditators intentionally skip this element so that they can challenge their minds and bodies.

Another optional element of meditation is a comfortable position. Whether you are walking, sitting, or laying down, you should feel comfortable in order to get the most out of your practice. You should never meditate in a position that feels painful, unsafe, or dangerous.

Finally, the last element of meditation is an open attitude. Like the focused attention element, it is impossible to meditate without an open attitude. This element will allow you to practice, challenge yourself, and grow without self-judgment and ridicule.

Meditation tools

As we have learned, there are different types of meditation. One way to distinguish these many techniques is through the use of tools.

The most popularly known meditation tool is postures or asanas. Asanas are used in both spiritual and non-spiritual meditations. They can include yoga postures, walking, or mindfully doing a task. Yoga classes, for example, use asanas as part of their meditative practices.

Another popular meditation tool is prayer beads. Prayer beads are used as tools of devotional meditation in spiritual settings such as Christianity, Gaudiya Vaishnavism, Buddhism, and Jainism. The meditator recites a mantra as each bead is counted and continues this until the entire mala or beaded chain is finished.

Meditation in the modern world

Since its conception in 150 BCE, meditation has changed drastically. Meditation was originally associated with religious thought in India and

China, but it eventually spread to Eastern Asian, Middle Eastern, and European religious practices too.

Once Asian meditative practices were shared with the West, Western traditions began to use meditation for non-religious purposes. As a result, many meditators today are non-religious and practice meditation for its health benefits. Still, a large number of people meditate for religious or spiritual purposes.

Since meditation has developed greatly, there are many types of meditative practices. Most of these practices can be classified as focused meditation or open-monitoring meditation. Within these two categories are countless meditation techniques, some of which use meditative tools like asanas or beads.

No matter the meditation category or type, though, meditation is viewed as a practice to deepen your mind's ability to focus and cause emotional stability and clarity. It incorporates elements like focused attention and an open mind for the betterment of the meditator.

CHAPTER 2
THE BENEFITS OF MEDITATION

THE BENEFITS OF MEDITATION

Many thinkers and scientists have been captivated by the health benefits of meditation. As a result, a number of studies and tests have been conducted to measure the impact of meditation on a person. These studies have found that meditation causes a number of benefits for both your body and mind.

Reduces stress

Today, many people experience chronic or severe stress, which is very negative to our overall well-being and health. Stress is our body's natural response to tense or dangerous situations. When you find yourself in these situations, your body releases hormones that prepare your natural flight or fight mentality.

Stress can be a good or bad thing, depending on the length of time that stress is experienced. Stress is good in short bursts because it can motivate us to accomplish our goals or finish tasks by their assigned deadlines. Long-term stress, though, is bad for our health because it can cause physical damage to our bodies and mind.

According to a number of studies, meditation is a great way to manage stress because it activates our body's relaxation response. This means that meditation restores the body to a calm state and undoes the effects of stress. As a result, meditation will allow you to manage your stress levels effectively and healthily.

Decreases symptoms of illness

According to the Mayo Clinic, meditation can be helpful if you are living with a medical condition. Anxiety, asthma, cancer, chronic pain, depression, heart disease, high blood pressure, IBS, sleep problems, and tension headaches are just a few of the illnesses that benefit from meditation.

Some researchers believe that meditation helps illnesses because they are exacerbated by stress. If stress is reduced, the symptoms of the illness can be reduced too. Since meditation increases relaxation, it reduces the symptoms of the illness.

Improves heart health

One of the best impacts of meditation on the body is that it improves heart health. According to the American Heart Association, patients who meditated saw a decrease in the thickness of their arterial walls. In contrast, patients who did not meditate experienced no change to their arterial walls.

The thickness of your arterial walls is very important. Thick arterial walls can cause a number of negative health issues such as high blood pressure, obesity, and other heart-related illnesses. If your arterial walls get too thick, they can impact the amount of blood that pumps from the heart, causing a heart attack or stroke.

With meditation, the thickness of the arterial wall decreases, which will allow your heart to pump blood more fluidly and decrease the chances of having a stroke or heart attack.

Decreases muscle tension

Another impact that meditation has on the body is decreasing muscle tension. Muscle tension is when the muscles are not relaxed properly, which often causes sharp pain and difficulty in moving. You may experience muscle tension if you work out intensely, experience severe stress, or take certain medications.

Since meditation often includes controlled breathing and calming the mind, it helps your muscles to relax as well. There is even a meditative technique, called Progressive Muscle Relaxation, that is targeted towards muscle relaxation.

More so, meditation reduces stress, which is a leading cause of muscle tension. If you reduce stress levels, you will also reduce its side effect of severe muscle tension.

Increases metabolism

Meditation also increases metabolism. Although meditation will not cause you to lose a ton of weight, it will help your body to burn off more calories while resting.

The reason for this is that meditation causes an increase of activity in the hypothalamus, the part of the brain that is responsible for controlling your metabolism. If this area is more active, then your body will naturally have a higher metabolism.

Slows the brain aging process

One way that meditation impacts the mind is that it better preserves the brain aging process. The brain aging process is measured by the amount of grey matter volume in the brain. The more grey matter, the better shape your brain is in in terms of aging.

A study conducted by UCLA found that long-term meditators had more grey matter volume than those who do not meditate. Younger meditators had more grey matter than older meditators, but older meditators had more grey matter than non-meditators of the same age. This study suggests that meditating slows the brain aging process.

Slowing the brain aging process is a great benefit of meditation. The longer the grey matter is preserved, the better your brain functions for muscle control, sensory perception, emotions, and self-control. So, meditation will allow us to use a well-functioning brain and mind for a longer part of our life.

Improves psychological well-being

Another way that meditation impacts the mind is that it changes the structure of the brain so that you experience an improvement in your psychological well-being. Brain structure is measured by the thickness of the cortical or the brain cell volume.

In a study conducted by Harvard Univeristy, researchers found that eight weeks of Mindfulness-Based Stress Reduction increases cortical thickness in the hippocampus and in areas that control emotion regulation and self-referential processing. At the same time, it decreases thickness in the amygdala, which controls fear, anxiety, and stress.

As a result, patients of the experiment reported an improvement in the psychological well-being and happiness. In fact, patients reported that they felt less stressed and generally felt better about themselves and their lives.

In other words, meditation affects the mind by resulting in increased happiness and contentment.

Additionally, meditation improves self-image and outlook. Studies have found that mindfulness meditation decreased depression in over 4,600 adults. One possible reason for this is that stress releases inflammatory chemicals called cytokines. Cytokines can affect mood and lead to depression. Since meditation manages stress, fewer cytokines are released, leading to a decrease in depression.

Some studies have even measured electrical activity in the brains of meditators. The study found that those who meditate have more activity in the regions of the brain that are associated with positive thinking and optimism, further showing how meditation improves one's psychological well-being.

Improves concentration

Meditation also improves one's concentration and ability to focus. In fact, some studies suggest that even a couple of weeks of meditation increases focus and memory.

In a study that measured the concentration benefits of meditation, those who meditated for a few weeks before the GRE experienced a 16-point increase in the overall score. This point increase is attributed to the increased ability to focus on the questions and test.

So, meditation increases one's ability to concentrate and focus. This increase affects the mind greatly because it increases its performance when tested and put under pressure.

Assists addicts in recovery

Addiction is a brutal disease that is difficult to regulate, control, and maintain. One way that some addicts have learned to control their addiction is through meditation. It is believed that meditation's effect on the self-control regions of the brain allows people to better control their addictions and impulses.

In one study, it was found that smokers who meditate were many times more likely to quit smoking than those who did not meditate. This study suggests that meditation helps addicts because it allows them to ride out the craving until it passes.

Other studies have looked at Mindfulness-Based Cognitive Therapy and Mindfulness-Based Relapse Prevention and found that meditation is effective at treating other forms of addiction as well.

CHAPTER 3
MEDITATION AND THE MIND

MEDITATION AND THE MIND

As we have seen, meditation has a great impact on the mind. Why is that? The simple answer is this: meditation enlarges regions of the brain associated with good behavior while it shrinks areas associated with bad behavior.

Left Hippocampus

The left hippocampus is the area of the brain that allows us to learn. Cognitive ability, memory, emotional regulators, self-awareness, and empathy are all related to the left hippocampus and its functionality.

The functionality of the hippocampus is measured based on the volume or grey-matter in the region. If the hippocampus has a lot of grey-matter, the person will experience more cognitive and empathetic abilities.

Meditation increases the volume of the left hippocampus. As a result, the meditator experiences an increase in cognitive ability, emotional regulation, self-awareness, and empathy, all of which are positive attributes.

Posterior Cingulate

The posterior cingulate is responsible for your wandering thoughts and sense of self. The larger the posterior cingulate, the more capable the person is at staying focused and having a realistic notion of the self.

Meditation increases the volume of the posterior cingulate, making it more functional. This results in enhanced concentration and a more fine-tuned sense of self. This fine-tuned sense of self is extremely important when talking about the mind since the mind is responsible for the understanding and projection of the self.

Without the mind, you would not have an understanding of yourself. Since meditation increases the part of the brain that regulates the self, meditation can allow your mind to more clearly conceive of your self and your place in the world.

Temporo Parietal Junction (TPJ)

The TPJ is the part of the brain that allows us to be empathetic and compassionate. More so, the TPJ is associated with our sense of perspective, which often allows us to be more compassionate and empathetic. When we put ourselves in another person's shoes, the TPJ becomes active.

Meditation increases the volume of the TPJ. Increasing the volume of TPJ allows us to become better people and achieve certain personal goals we set for ourselves.

As a result, meditation allows us to take the image we have for ourselves and turn it into reality.

Amygdala

The amygdala is responsible for feelings of anxiety, fear, and stress. It is responsible for fight or flight behaviors whenever we find ourselves in stressful, confrontational, or dangerous situations. In certain situations, the amygdala can save our lives, but it often causes unnecessary stress, which is unhealthy and damaging to our well-being.

Unlike the other parts of the brain, the amygdala shrinks after meditation. When the amygdala shrinks, you experience less anxiety and stress, which allows you to feel more positively about yourself and your situations. As your amygdala shrinks, you experience an increase in your psychological well-being.

Putting it all together

Once again, meditation causes the left hippocampus, posterior cingulate, and TPJ to expand, while it causes the amygdala to shrink. As a result, meditators experience more cognitive function, emotion regulation, concentration, realistic notions of the self, and compassion. All the while, they experience less fear, anxiety, and stress.

These effects allow for your mind to function in a way that is more efficient, gentle, and conducive to a healthy and happy life. In other words, meditation has a positive impact on the mind in that it makes it work in a way that improves your intellect, memory, concentration, and emotional well-being.

CHAPTER 4
MEDITATION AND THE BODY

MEDITATION AND THE BODY

Meditation also has a large impact on the body. In fact, meditation does a great job of balancing your body and its functions. The reason for this is that meditation activates the body's relaxation response, which has a number of positive ramifications.

How meditation affects the body

As previously stated, meditation activates your body's relaxation response, but what exactly is this? During the relaxation response, your body begins to become physiologically relaxed. This means that your blood pressure, heart rate, digestive functioning, and hormone levels return to normal after a state of stress.

Part of the reason that all your functions return to normal is that harmful hormones are reduced whenever you start relaxing. Whenever your body detects stress, it produces cortisol. Cortisol is helpful in short-bursts but can disrupt sleep-cycles, create a negative mood, and make you feel tired over time. Relaxation reduces the chances of high-cortisol levels.

Additionally, your body's relaxation response allows you to turn off autopilot induced by stress. With your autopilot turned off, you can use your conscious mind and somatic nervous system to make changes in the automatic nervous system, which controls your heart rate, breathing rate, blood pressure, and hormones.

Putting it all together

Meditation allows your body to activate its relaxation response. When your relaxation response is activated, your body reduces its cortisol production, turns off its autopilot, and allows you to become physiologically relaxed, which protects your body from damage.

Imagine that your body is like car brakes. If you constantly slam on the brake pedal or ride with the emergency brake on, the brakes and brake pad will be worn out quickly. Your body is the same way.

If your body never experiences physiological relaxation, it will wear out much quicker. Meditation incites physiological relaxation, which will allow your body to be healthier for a longer period of time.

CHAPTER 5
CALMING THE MIND AND THE BODY

CALMING THE MIND AND THE BODY

One of the biggest benefits of meditation is that it calms both the mind and the body. Though this may seem like an easy task, very few activities calm both.

Benefits of calming the mind and body at the same time

Beyond the many benefits listed earlier, there are many other benefits of meditation, especially related to the fact that it calms the mind and the body at the same time.

Think about a time you were laying in bed, felt very tired, but you couldn't shut your mind. Or, think about the last time your body felt jittery, though your brain hurt, and you wanted nothing more than to sleep.

These are both instances where the mind and body are not working together, and you would have benefited from a meditative practice to bring your mind and body together as one.

The main benefit of calming the mind and body at once is that it allows you to experience full relaxation. From every angle, your being is allowed to relax and feel the benefits of its relaxation response.

Another benefit of calming the mind and body is that it helps you to create a more holistic understanding of the self. Many people feel detached from their bodies, or they feel like their minds and bodies are not in sync. Calming the mind and body forces you to conjoin your mind and body, which creates a complete notion of the self.

How to calm the mind and body

Calming the mind and body as one requires you to use both for a single purpose. If you don't use both your mind and body, you run the risk of one not calming down.

You can begin to calm your mind and body by intentionally slowing your breath. It is important to use your mind to focus and control the breath. You may want to do this by using breathing techniques. A popular breathing technique includes inhaling for 4 seconds, holding the breath for 5 seconds, and exhaling for 7 seconds.

As you breathe, begin to imagine all the energy-draining from your body with every exhale. See if you can feel the weight in your body, and try to imagine that your body is getting heavier. Continue to do this until you feel your body relax. At that point, allow your brain to fully relax as well.

The reason that this technique works is because it takes a bodily process, namely your breath, and connects it with your mind in a way that is conducive to a relaxing setting. If you only focus on your thoughts or only focus on your breath, you will not get the full benefits of this technique.

Calming the mind and body separately

There may be times when you may want to focus on calming one but not the other. When you feel overwhelmed at work, for example, you may want to quiet your mind without tiring your body. Or, when you feel tired in bed but can't get your mind to shut off, you may want to focus on calming the mind.

Overall, it is very hard to calm one without the other. When you calm your mind, your body begins to calm as a side effect, and vice versa. So, you will probably calm both when you meditate.

If one is already calmed, though, you can focus to make both calm. Take the laying in bed example again. You are laying in bed and feel physically tired, but you can't shut off your brain. In this case, you should focus on controlling your mind and joining it with your body.

CHAPTER 6
MEDITATION IN MOVEMENT

MEDITATION IN MOVEMENT

Many people imagine meditation as being boring, quiet, and still. Though some meditation practices look like this, there are other forms of meditation that are almost the opposite. One type of meditation that contradicts this view of meditation is movement meditation.

What is movement meditation?

Movement meditation is when you move through various postures or movements with a mindful and slow pace. The key to movement meditation is being mindful when you move. If your movements lack mindfulness, then you are simply moving.

Movement meditation is great for connecting your mind and body. If you struggle with identity or feeling like you belong in the world, movement meditation may be a meditation technique that might help.

Being mindful while you move may be weird at first, but you will soon get used to it as you practice. You can begin by thinking about how your body feels. Do any muscles hurt? What feels good? Can you feel your breath? These sorts of questions can help you draw awareness to yourself in a mindful way.

You can also draw attention to how things interact with your body. Feel the floor. Is it hard or soft? Hot or cold? These questions can help you feel grounded in your world and better understand your relationship with it.

Movement meditation in practice

Once you become comfortable with being attuned with your body and world, you can begin to do movement meditations. These meditations will take a lot of practice and work to execute perfectly, so be kind to yourself and allow yourself to make mistakes.

You should begin your movement meditations by sitting comfortably and paying attention to the breath. Once you feel comfortable, put your hands on your body, and feel your hands move with your breath.

From here, you can do any movement you like. One popular movement is standing up. Feel how your muscles move and support your weight. As you stand up, go at your own pace and listen to your body.

Once you are standing up, feel your feet firmly in the ground. Try to activate your legs and core while placing your weight on all four corners of your feet. This stance will feel awkward at first, but try to fight through the feeling.

Reach up with one hand like you are picking fruit. Notice how your shoulders extend as your elbow straightens. Is there any tension? How does your blood flow feel going up your arm? Now repeat with your other arm.

Once you are ready, put both hands down and start to move around the room. You can move in any way you like. Notice how your legs feel now that they are no longer activated. After moving for a bit, sit back down and compare how you felt at the beginning to how you feel now.

Popular Asanas

An asana is a body posture that involves sitting in some way. Yoga classes are often a series of asanas strung together in a flow. Asanas can be a great way to practice movement meditations, especially if you want to challenge the strength, endurance, or flexibility of your body.

One of the most popular asanas is adho, or downward-facing dog. Downward dog is when your hands and feet are on the ground while your back is extended and hips reaching upwards. You can get in downward dog by going to a plank position. From there, leave your hands and feet where they are, but lift your hips backward and upwards.

Another popular asana is balasana, or child's pose. Child's pose is when you are folded over your thighs. You can get in child's pose by sitting on your heels, and then folding over until your chest rests on your thighs. You can choose to put your hands above or behind you.

Shavasana is another popular asana. Shavasana is known as corpse pose because it involves laying on your back with your arms and legs extended and relaxed, much like a corpse. This pose is easy enough to get into, but it can be difficult to remain mindful during, making it a difficult pose.

When doing asanas, you can either do one asana at a time, or you can string asanas together to create a flow. Either way, it is crucial to stay attuned and mindful of your body. Asanas without mindfulness are just motions.

CHAPTER 7
MEDITATION BY OBSERVATION

MEDITATION BY OBSERVATION

Another form of meditation is through observation. Observation meditation includes observing yourself, your thoughts, and the world around you. Whenever you practice observation meditation, you self reflect and view yourself in relation to the world around you.

What is observation meditation?

Though it is a common myth that meditation requires shutting your mind, many people view meditation as the art of observing your thoughts. Whenever you observe your thoughts in meditation, you allow your mind to relax and meld with your body.

In short, observation meditation is whenever you meditate to your observational thoughts. Though this may seem odd, it is very common and utilizes your stream of thought for meditative purposes, combatting the myth that meditation requires emptying your mind.

When you observe your stream of thought, you observe the way your body feels and your interaction with the world. You should observe things like muscle tension, breath, the feel of the floor, the feel of the air, and anything that affects your senses. You can make these observations either through mindfulness or positive self-talk.

Either way, observation meditation just entails using your senses to observe yourself and the world.

Benefits of observation meditation

Observation meditation is beneficial for a number of reasons. Notably, observational meditation encourages positive self-talk. Positive self-talk is when you acknowledge your feelings and don't judge yourself for them. Many people get in the habit of ridiculing their own thoughts, but observation meditation does the opposite.

Whenever you practice positive self-talk, you are more likely to have an optimistic mindset and view of the world. As a result, you experience a happier well being.

Another benefit of observation meditation is that it sharpens your focus. Humans think all the time, but we seldom think about our thoughts, and we let them aimlessly wander, instead. Observation meditation forces us to focus on our own thoughts, which then increases our ability to focus.

A third benefit of observation meditation is that you get to know yourself better. Everyone knows that the best way to get to know someone is to talk to them and find out what they think about things. The same goes for yourself: you can get to know yourself better by listening to your own thoughts.

Though knowing yourself may seem ridiculous, very few people are aware of their feelings and triggers, which causes them to lash out or feel hurt without ever knowing why. When you get to know yourself, you become aware of these things, giving you the power to make changes and grow as a person.

How to practice observation meditation

As stated previously, observation meditation involves observing your thoughts and feelings in a mindful way. There are many instances in which you can do this, so feel free to practice observation meditation at different points in your day.

Here is a common observation meditation practice:

Begin by sitting in a comfortable seated position. Close your eyes, and place your hands on your legs. Draw attention to your breath, and begin to slow it down. As your breath slows, pay attention to how you feel when you breathe, the temperature of the air, and anything else related to the breath.

As you become more aware of your breath, allow yourself to start focusing on other parts of the body as well. Do your hands feel awkward on your legs? Is the floor cold? How do your knees feel if they're bent? Ask questions like these so that you become aware of how your body feels at the moment.

Once you feel that you have adequately observed your physical body, allow your brain to wander. Take note of the thoughts that come into your head. Instead of quickly dismissing them, listen to them, and then let them go. As your thought goes, you may find that another thought pops into your head. Do the same for this thought as well.

You can think about your thoughts for as long as you would like. Whenever you are finished, bring your attention back to the body. Does it feel any different than it did at the beginning? If so, note how.

At this point, you may want to move your body a bit. You can extend your legs out, raise your arms, lay down, or stand up. Just do whatever feels right to your body. If you feel any tension, for instance, you may want to stretch out that muscle.

No matter what movement you choose, pay attention to how the body feels. Take note of how the muscles contract and move and how differently they feel then they did when you were seated. Do not just move around. Truly think about how your body feels and observe the way it moves.

Once you feel that you have adequately moved, you should gently bring yourself back to a seated or laid position. Close your eyes, and begin to focus on your breath again. Observe your breath and your thoughts one last time. Gently begin to open your eyes bye cracking your eyelids open a little bit at a time. Observe how the light feels.

Once your eyes are completely opened, the practice is finished. Even though the practice is over, you can still incorporate observation meditation Into your day or night. Whenever you feel a pain or are letting your mind wander, check-in with yourself.

Checking in throughout the day is a fast and easy way to practice observation meditation without rearranging your schedule. You can do this whether you're sitting at your desk, waiting in line, or driving to work.

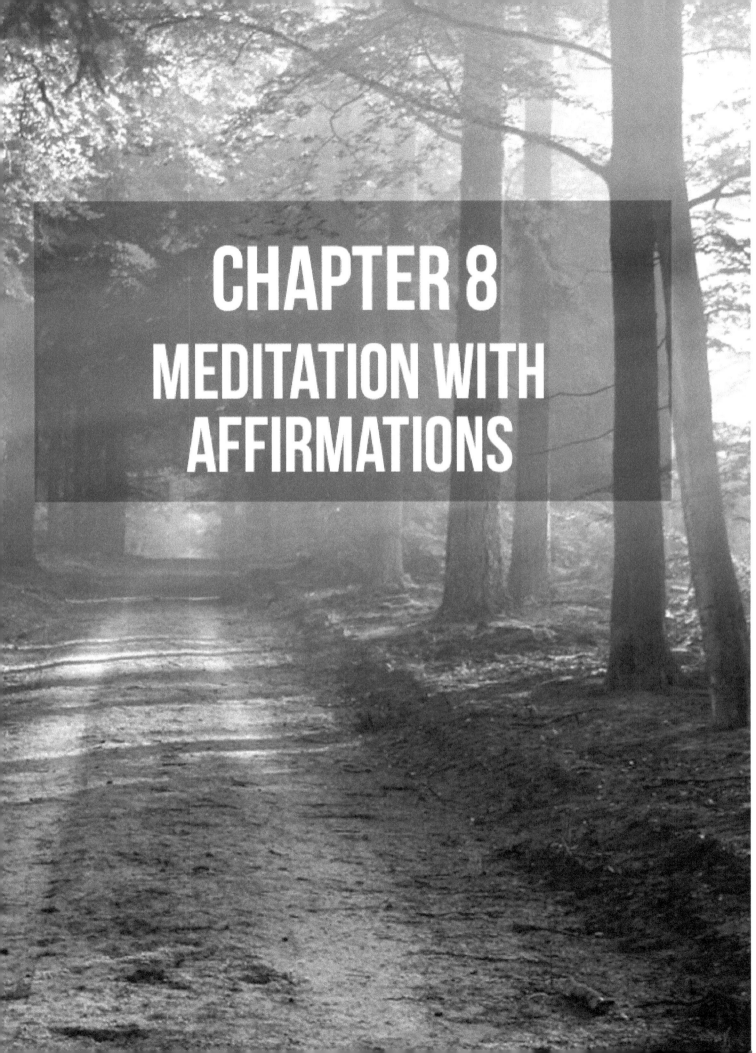

CHAPTER 8
MEDITATION WITH AFFIRMATIONS

MEDITATION WITH AFFIRMATIONS

If you have ever been to a yoga class, you've probably heard of creating an affirmation for your practice. For many new meditators, creating an affirmation and using that affirmation can be extremely confusing and feel unrewarding. If this is your experience with affirmations, you are not alone.

What are affirmations?

Affirmations are sentences that we say to ourselves or others in order to create a conscious and subconscious mind that affects our behavior, thinking, habits, and environment.

As we repeat these affirmations to ourselves, the ideas and associated images with that affirmation become engraved in our conscious and subconscious mind. As a result, the affirmation changes our behavior, habits, actions, and reactions in accordance with the affirmation.

Here are some popular affirmations:

- My past does not determine my future.

- I am capable of making my own decisions.

- I control how I react to others.

- I'm worthy of love.

- I don't need anyone else to feel happiness.

- My imperfections make me special.

- I have the power to create change.

- I am enough.

- My needs and wants are important.

- I attract money.

- I will accomplish my goals.

Benefits of meditation with affirmations

Meditating with affirmations results in a number of benefits for your body and mind.

One benefit of meditating with affirmations is that they motivate you to accomplish your goal. The reason that they motivate you is that they give you a clear idea of what you want, and they allow your mind to stay focused on that goal.

Another benefit of meditating with affirmations is that they change the way you think and behave. The affirmations themselves are not powerful or magical, but your recitation allows them to affect the way you think. As a result, you are more likely to do things that result in the accomplishment of your goal.

Finally, meditating with affirmations makes you feel better. Saying positive things to yourself increases your self-worth, self-image, and outlook on the world. As a result, you will feel more positive, energetic, and optimistic about yourself and your life.

How to create affirmations

If you have never tried meditating with an affirmation before, you may be wondering how to pick out an affirmation. Affirmations are easy to make because you can either find them on the Internet or use your own feelings to create your own.

If you want to test drive affirmations, you can look online for affirmation ideas. Simply type "affirmation ideas" into your search engine, and you'll find countless of affirmations for you to try out.

If you want, you can even try to create your own affirmations. It may feel awkward at first, but creating your own affirmations ensures that they match what you want out of your life and are personal to your needs and desires.

To create your own affirmations, begin by thinking about what you need in your life. You may want to practice observation meditation in order to understand the way you feel and the things you want out of life.

You may also want to make a vision board. A vision board is a physical poster board, paper, or Pinterest board that represents all your goals and wishes for the near future.

For your affirmations, you should focus on mid- to long-term goals. Monthly goals are the perfect goal lengths because they allow enough time for the affirmation to work while still being soon enough that you see a light at the end of the tunnel.

Once you have a clear idea of where you're at in life and what you want out of it, you can start to form your own affirmations. You will want the affirmations to be tailored to your exact needs.

For example, if you are struggling to make ends meet, your affirmation may be, "I am smart and capable of providing for myself and my loved ones."

This affirmation speaks to the described scenario while giving it a positive spin.

When you are creating your affirmation, you want it to be focused and not too wordy. If it is not focused, the affirmation will not be as effective because your mind will be clouded with its many parts. The same goes if the sentence is wordy; it will be hard to remember.

Once you have your affirmations, you can begin to meditate with them.

How to meditate with affirmations

Meditating with affirmations is relatively easy. The key is that you are consistent with your affirmations. Reciting your affirmations inconsistently will not result in the end products you want.

If you are new to affirmations, you can begin by sprinkling them into your daily routine. It is best to say your affirmations twice a day. Say your first affirmation as soon as you wake up in the morning. Saying your first affirmation will set the day on a right note and motivate you to accomplish your tasks for the day.

Many people find remembering to say their morning affirmation Difficult when they first start out. In order to remember to say your affirmation, you can either put a sticky note on your mirror or set your alarm title on your phone as the affirmation.

Your second affirmation should be said right before you go to bed. Saying your affirmation before sleep helps you rest your mind so that way you can sleep more soundly and not have as disruptive dreams.

Once you get in the groove of saying your affirmations morning and night, you should also incorporate intentional meditation affirmation practices into your day. Start by having a 5-minute session. During the session, say all of your affirmations at least 10 times in a slow, relaxing, and confident voice.

As you say your affirmations, attempt to imagine them coming true. This creates a vision in your head of what you want this affirmation to look like in practice. Doing this will keep your mind focused as well as create focused images of your affirmations.

CHAPTER 9
CREATING A DAILY PRACTICE

CREATING A DAILY PRACTICE

Now that you have seen all the benefits and types of meditation, you may be wondering how to start meditating in a way to see lasting results in your life. In short, the most effective way to meditate in order to experience all these benefits is to create a daily practice.

A daily practice is a meditation session that you do every day, ideally at the same time every day. This session will get you in a set routine, give you a time to relax, and recur enough that you will benefit from the meditations.

How do I create a daily practice?

Daily practices are easy enough to create. Begin by choosing a time of day that you would like to meditate. Many people choose to meditate either in the morning or at night. Both times come with notable benefits.

Meditating in the morning will start your day on a good note and motivate you to accomplish and stay focused on your tasks. This time may be ideal for you if you need help finding motivation or have extra time in the morning.

In contrast, meditating at night will give you a chance to reflect on the day and work out any unresolved feelings before you go to bed. This will help you sleep easier and feel more prepared for the next day. You may want to meditate at night if you have trouble sleeping, need more time to self reflect, or hate getting up early.

If you are really motivated to start meditating, you can always meditate in the morning and night. Just make sure that you do not overwhelm yourself because this may cause you to forgo meditation altogether.

After you decide when you want to meditate, you should also decide on the length of time for your practice. Meditating for the same amount of time trains your brain to focus under a time constraint. It is recommended that your daily practice lasts anywhere from 5-minutes to an hour, depending on your needs.

Although you should aim for your daily sessions to last around the same amount of time each day, you can always adjust the time later on or make certain sessions last longer or shorter than others. This time commitment that you were deciding on now is not a hard and fast rule. Simply think of it more as a guideline or suggestion for yourself.

Next, you may want to set up or decide on a daily practice area for you to meditate in. This may be a small corner of your living room or a yoga mat in your office. No matter what, you want to create a safe space so that way your mind immediately goes on meditation mode for your daily practice.

After that, you should settle on a go-to meditation technique. Having a go-to meditation technique will save you time and energy on days that you're tired or don't feel like meditating.

Having a go-to technique does not mean that your daily practice has to be that meditation style every single time. Your daily practice should reflect your daily needs while being rooted in routine. So, some days you may choose to do your go-to meditation technique, while other days you may choose a different technique.

Doing your daily practice

Once you have decided on what your daily meditation practice looks like, it's time to start doing your daily practice. Here are some things to remember about doing your daily practice.

Try to do daily practice at the same time and for the same minimum length every single day. This will train your brain to get in the groove of your meditation and allow it to do its work.

Additionally, remember that every day is different. While sticking to your schedule is ideal, improvisation is good too. Change up your technique, meditate longer, or even rearrange your meditation space. Improvisation based on your daily needs is always encouraged because it ensures that your meditation is relevant and helpful to your present life.

Finally, be kind to yourself. There will come a day when you either forget or don't have the time to do your daily meditation practice. When this day comes, do not beat yourself up. Be kind to yourself and gently remind yourself to start back on your daily meditation schedule the next day.

CHAPTER 10
DAILY MEDITATION FOR THE SOUL

DAILY MEDITATION FOR THE SOUL

Many adults find their soul and spirit dulled and disconnected from their bodies and lives. One way to get back in touch with and reinvigorate your soul is through daily meditations. Here is a daily meditation that will help you foster your relationship with your soul.

Journal meditation

One of the best ways to meditate for your soul is through Journal meditation. Journal meditation is very similar to observation meditation in that it utilizes your observations about yourself. It differs from observation meditation in that it comes with specific prompts, and you write down your observations, as opposed to just thinking them.

The first prompt for your journal meditation is "Today, I am thankful for..." You can list as few or as many things as you would like after the prompt.

The second prompt is "What do I need right now?" This question may seem silly, but very few people take the time to ask themselves what they need at the present moment.

You begin by asking yourself the prompts and reflecting on your answers. Stay keenly aware of your feelings and observe how your thoughts wander around the prompt. Do not feel embarrassed about where your mind goes.

Once you have observed your thoughts in response to the prompts, write down your answers. Writing down the answers is a crucial step. It allows you to see a physical representation of your soul. Don't worry about spelling, format, or handwriting. Just write what your soul tells you to write.

Once you have answered both of these prompts truthfully and adequately, you should reflect on the journals. Think about why you may have written these answers and continue to enjoy your connectivity to your own soul.

Though this is not a requirement for the meditation, many people find doing a journal meditation in the morning to be extremely helpful. It allows them to start their day on a good note and do their daily tasks with their soul meditation in mind.

CONCLUSION

As we have learned, meditation is a practice that results in a number of positive benefits to your mental and physical well-being. The reason for this is that meditation incites the relaxation response in your mind and body, which results in a number of positive effects.

More importantly, we learned that meditation does not have to be that time-consuming, allowing anyone to practice meditation. Regardless of whether you prefer to meditate in movement, by observation, or with affirmations, you should be able to incorporate your favorite meditation techniques into a daily practice to feed your soul and experience the full benefits of meditation.

MEDITATION
FOR
BUSY PEOPLE

CHECKLIST

CHECKLIST

- Defining meditation
  - Practice
    - Train attention and achieve mental clarity
  - History
    - Practiced since 1500 BCE
    - Early meditation practiced in early Hinduism
    - Early meditation practiced in early Buddhism
    - Early meditation practiced in early Judaism
    - Early meditation practiced in early Christianity
    - Early meditation practiced in early Islam
    - Non-spiritual meditation in the 18th century
  - Categories
    - Focused meditation
    - Open monitoring meditation
  - Elements
    - Focused attention
    - Relaxed breathing
    - Quiet setting
    - Comfortable position
    - Open attitude
  - Tools
    - Postures or asanas
    - Prayer beads

- Benefits of meditation
  - Reduces stress
  - Decreases symptoms of illness
  - Improves heart health
  - Decreases muscle tension
  - Increases metabolism
  - Slows brain aging
  - Improves psychological wellbeing
  - Improves concentration
  - Assists addicts in recovery

- Meditation and the mind
  - Left hippocampus grows
    - Increases cognitive ability
    - Increases memory
    - Increases emotional regulation
    - Increases self-awareness
    - Increases empathy
  - Posterior cingulate grows
    - Regulates notion of the self
    - Enhances concentration
  - Temporo parietal junction grows
    - Increases empathy
  - Amygdala shrinks
    - Reduces fear
    - Reduces anxiety
    - Reduces anger

- Meditation and the body
  - Activates relaxation response
    - Reduces cortisol
    - Turns off autopilot

- Calming the mind and the body
  - Benefits
    - Experience full relaxation
    - Holistic view of the self
  - How to
    - Slow breath
    - Focus mind on controlling breath
    - Practice breathing techniques
    - Imagine energy leaving body
    - Imagine body getting heavier
    - Allow body to relax
    - Focus until mind and body relax

- Meditation in movement
  - Definition
    - Meditating to movement
  - How to
    - Sit comfortably
    - Slow breath
    - Focus mind on controlling breath
    - Think about your body
    - Think about how your body interacts with the world around you
    - Begin to move with eyes closed if possible
    - Stand up
    - Think about muscles contracting
    - Feel feet firmly on the ground
    - Lift up arm
    - Think about how it feels
    - Put both hands down
    - Move around the room
    - Pay attention to your body
    - Sit back down
    - Sit comfortably
    - Open eyes
  - Popular postures
    - Downward-facing dog
    - Child's pose
    - Corpse pose

- Meditation by observation
  - Definition
    - Meditation to observational thoughts
    - Observe stream of thought
  - Benefits
    - Encourages positive self-talk
    - Increases optimistic mindset
    - Increases happier wellbeing
    - Sharpens focus
    - Get to know yourself better

- o How to
  - Sit comfortably
  - Close eyes
  - Focus mind on controlling breath
  - Slow breath
  - Focus on other parts of the body
  - Pay attention to how your body feels
  - Allow brain to wander
  - Recognize your thoughts
  - Let thought finish
  - Gently let go of thought
  - Do this until you're ready to finish
  - Bring attention back to the breath
  - Slowly open eyes

- Meditation with affirmations
  - o Affirmations
    - Positive sentences we say to ourselves or others
    - Associate affirmation with images
  - o Benefits
    - Increases motivation
    - Changes behavior
    - Changes habits
    - Changes actions
    - Changes reactions
  - o Create affirmations
    - Search online for ideas
    - Practice observation meditation
    - Ask yourself what you want
    - Ask yourself what you need
    - Think about your goals
    - Focus on mid- to long-term goals
    - Form affirmation

- How to
  - Repeat affirmations morning and night
  - Practice meditation with affirmations
  - Sit comfortably
  - Close eyes
  - Focus mind on breath
  - Say affirmations out loud
  - Repeat 10 times
  - Focus mind back on breath
  - Open eyes

- Creating a daily practice
  - How to
    - Select time of day
    - Select meditation length
    - Create a meditation space
    - Create go-to meditation
  - Tips
    - Improvise
    - Be kind to yourself
    - Allow yourself to mess up

- Daily meditation for the soul
  - Journal meditation
    - Observation meditation with journaling
    - Ask yourself, "What am I thankful for today?"
    - Reflect
    - Write down answer
    - Ask yourself, "What do I need right now?"
    - Reflect
    - Write down answer

MEDITATION
FOR
BUSY PEOPLE

RESOURCE CHEAT SHEET

Debunking Myths about Meditation

- o "11 Meditation Myths You Should Stop Believing," *Forbes*
- o "7 Myths About Meditation Preventing You From Grasping the Amazing Benefits of Mindfulness," *Inc.*
- o "5 Myths About Meditation," *Yoga International*
- o "Debunking Myths Around Meditation" *Beyond Blue*
- o "12 Myths About Meditation We Have To Stop Believing," *HuffPost*

Meditation When You're Busy

- o "The Mindfulness Guide for People Too Busy to Meditate," *Psycom*
- o "How to Squeeze meditation into Your Busy Schedule," *The Chopra Center*
- o "7 Easy Ways To Meditate with a Busy Schedule," *The Chopra Center*
- o "If You're Too Busy to Meditate, Read This," *Harvard Business Review*
- o "How to Meditate If You Have a Busy Life," *Life with Confidence*

Understanding Meditation

- o "Understanding Meditation," *The Art of Living*
- o "What is Meditation?" *Insider*
- o "What is Meditation?" *The Buddhist Centre*
- o "Meditation Definition" *Mind Works*
- o "The Meeting of Meditation Disciplines and Western Psychology" by Roger Walsh and Shauna Shapiro

History of Meditation

- o "A Brief History of Meditation," *Mind Works*
- o "The History and Origin of Meditation," *PositivePsychology.com*
- o "Meditation History," *News Medical*
- o "How Meditation Went Mainstream," *Time*
- o "An Overview of Meditation: Its Origins and Traditions," *Psychology Today*

Benefits of Meditation

- "Meditation: A Simple, Fast Way to Reduce Stress," *Mayo Clinic*
- "12 Science-Based Benefits of Meditation," *Health Line*
- "Meditation: In Depth," *National Center for Complementary and Integrative Health*
- "When Science Meets Mindfulness," *The Harvard Gazette*
- "7 Ways Meditation Can Actually Change the Brain," *Forbes*
- "3 Ways Meditation Can Help Your Heart, Body and Mind," *Penn Medicine*

Meditation and the Mind

- "How Meditation Changes the Brain," *Mind Works*
- "7 Ways Meditation Can Actually Change the Brain," *Forbes*
- "Harvard Neuroscientist: Meditation Not Only Reduces Stress, Here's How it Changes Your Brain," *The Washington Post*
- "LOOK: What Meditation Can Do For Your Mind, Body and Spirit," *HuffPost*
- "This Is Your Brain on Meditation," *Psychology Today*

Meditation and the Body

- "How Does Meditation Affect the Body?" *Gaiam*
- "Meditation Balances the Body's Systems," *WebMD*
- "Meditation: In Depth," *National Center for Complementary and Integrative Health*
- "Meditation: A Simple, Fast Way to Reduce Stress," *Mayo Clinic*
- "Five Ways Mindfulness Meditation is Good for Your Health," UC Berkeley's GGSC

Calming the Mind and the Body

- o "Stress Management: Relaxing your Mind and Body," *University of Michigan Medicine*
- o "12 Quick Mini-Meditation to Calm Your Mind and Body," *Psychology Today*
- o "Meditation: A Simple, Fast Way to Reduce Stress," *Mayo Clinic*
- o "4 Calming Meditation Techniques," *Gaiam*
- o "A Sequence to Calm Your Mind Before Meditation," *Yoga International*

Meditation in Movement

- o "What is Movement Meditation?" *American Institute of Health Care Professionals*
- o "Movement Meditation: Centering Breath," *Yoga Journal*
- o "Movement Based Meditation," *Totally Meditation*
- o "Mindful Movement Meditation," *Dummies: a Willey Brand*
- o "5 Movement Meditation Practices That'll Work Your Body and Clear Your Mind," *Fit Bottomed Girls*

Meditation by Observation

- o "A Meditation on Observing Thoughts, Non-Judgmentally," *Mindful*
- o "Self-Observation," *InsightTimer* (music and talks for self-observation)
- o "Observation and Meditation," *theo*
- o "Intro to Meditation – The Challenge of Self Observation," *HuffPost*
- o "Meditation Observation," teaching assignment by Dr. Matt King
- o "True Meditation is the Science of Observing Your Thoughts," *Big Think*

Meditation with Affirmations

- o "How to Create Affirmations and Use Them During Meditation," blog by Rachael Kable
- o "Meditation Positive Affirmations," *Free Affirmations*
- o "How to Use Affirmations," *The Guided Meditation Site*
- o "Positive Daily Affirmations: Is There Science Behind It?" *PositivePsychology.com*
- o "Daily Affirmations," *Audible* (guided meditations with affirmations)

Creating a Daily Practice

- o "How to Begin a Daily Meditation Practice," *experience L!fe*
- o "How to Meditate Daily," *zen habits*
- o "8 Steps to Establish a Daily Meditation Practice," *The Chopra Center*
- o "How to Make Meditation a Daily Habit," *Mindful*
- o "Create Your Own Meditation Space," *AARP*

Daily Meditation for the Soul

- o "Get In Touch With Your Soul With This Daily Meditation Ritual," *daily life*
- o "Meditation: A Conversation With Your Soul," *LBM with Carol Millar*
- o "A Common Meditation for All Souls," *All Souls: A Unitarian Universalist Congregation*
- o "Daily Meditation: Replenish Your Soul," *HuffPost*
- o "Speak with Your Soul – Guided Meditation Audio," *The Daily Positive*

CPSIA information can be obtained
at www.ICGtesting.com
Printed in the USA
BVHW051549110121
597542BV00012B/991